ISBN 978-1-332-86416-4
PIBN 10270705

PREFACE

IT is with much pleasure that we present a revised and enlarged edition of our practical book on wood finishing. The earlier issues were so well received that we believe this will meet with still wider favor, containing as it does new matter of interest to both architects and wood-finishers. We have endeavored to be practical, eliminating all matter having no direct bearing on the subject treated.

There is nothing experimental in the methods given for the various styles of wood finishing. They are all based upon actual experience and may be relied upon as being correct.

While the use of Berry Brothers' varnishes, wood finishes and other products, makes possible the very best results in the way of a finish, whatever of value may be found in the hints and directions given herein, is in no way impaired because we suggest the use of Berry Brothers' Finishes. The staining, shellacing, filling, etc., as the case may be, are the necessary preludes to a successful finish, whatever varnishes may be used to finish with, and the mode of applying and manipulating, all interior varnishes is substantially the same.

We trust our book may serve as a useful reference for the architect in writing his specifications, and also that it may not be devoid of interest to our good friends the Decorators and Wood Finishers.

INDEX

WHAT TO USE

LUXEBERRY WOOD FINISH.

(TRADE MARK.)

————

THIS is for general interior work, and is unequalled for producing a handsome and durable finish on all woods. It develops and preserves the grain, and can either be left in the natural gloss or rubbed and polished, as may be desired.

LUXEBERRY WOOD FINISH *"White"* is very pale and can be used on the lightest woods without discoloring them in the least, while the *"light"* is suitable for Oak, Ash, Chestnut and similar woods.

Where an especially fine finish is wanted, we recommend LUXEBERRY WOOD FINISH *"White"* on **any** wood, as it is an exceptionally nice article and well repays the additional cost per gallon.

LUXEBERRY WOOD FINISH is a new name for genuine Hard Oil Finish, of which we are the originators and sole manufacturers.

So many worthless varnishes are now offered, wrongfully called Hard Oil Finish, that we have decided to put out our standard grades of Hard Oil Finish as LUXEBERRY WOOD FINISH *"White"* or *"Light"* under which name the consumer may hereafter depend upon getting Berry Brothers' genuine Hard Oil Finish, upon which we have built up an international reputation.

The word "Luxeberry" is derived from "Luxe," meaning highest quality, joined to our name, the compound word "Luxeberry" being our duly registered trade mark.

The specification of "LUXEBERRY WOOD FINISH" ("White" or "Light") will tend to check imposition and do much toward affording protection against the evils resulting from the use of poor or unsuitable varnish on the woodwork, and we hope all who are friendly to the use of Berry Brothers' Hard Oil Finish will adopt the new name to our mutual interest.

This change of name need not result in any complications, as it simply necessitates writing for Berry Brothers' White Hard Oil Finish, "LUXEBERRY WOOD FINISH" (*"White"*) and for Berry Brothers' Light Hard Oil Finish, "LUXEBERRY WOOD FINISH" (*"Light."*)

LIQUID GRANITE.

(TRADE MARK.)

———

T HE practice of dispensing with carpets and finishing floors in natural woods has become so popular that an imperative demand has arisen for a "Finish" possessing greater elasticity and wearing properties than any ordinary varnish.

Liquid Granite is devised to meet this want; it is an entirely reliable article for use on parquetry and natural wood floors, combining as it does the three great requisites in a floor finish, elasticity, toughness and durability.

Being transparent it will not obscure the grain of the wood, but will develop its beauty and preserve it.

It will be found superior to any preparation of wax, being more easily applied, more economical to use and making a much more durable finish.

Liquid Granite is so tough that although wood finished with it will dent under a blow, the finish will give with it without cracking.

There are in the market a large number of articles called floor finish; THERE IS BUT ONE LIQUID GRANITE, the name being a registered trade mark, and once used it will be used always, as it is the only perfect floor finish made.

ELASTIC OUTSIDE FINISH.

———

THIS is intended for store fronts, outside doors, and other purposes, where the exposure is excessive, and will be found superior to any thing of the kind hitherto offered.

It is made with special reference to durability under exposure to the weather, dries dust-free quickly, and will make either a dead or a brilliant finish. The official reports made on tests by the Master House Painters' and Decorators' Association of the United States on twenty-four different makes of outside varnishes, not only commended our ELASTIC OUTSIDE FINISH, but showed it to dry dust-proof quicker than any other commended outside varnish tested

The value of this feature is apparent.

ELASTIC INTERIOR FINISH.

———

T HIS is intended for such interior work as is subjected to severe exposure or usage. It has many of the characteristics of Luxeberry Wood Finish, and is tougher and somewhat slower drying. It possesses great elasticity, combined with unusual durability and will resist the action of hot water, soap, etc., longer than anything else we know of. It is peculiarly adapted for use on window sash and sills, bath rooms, inside blinds, etc., and is also especially suitable for such portions of the interior wood-work as are to be left with an unrubbed varnish finish.

We confidently offer ELASTIC INTERIOR FINISH as the best article of its kind yet introduced.

SHINGLETINT.

(TRADE MARK.)

———

S HINGLE STAINS need no introduction. The artistic effects produced by their use is well understood, as well as their preservative properties, when they are scientifically made.

SHINGLETINT represents the highest result yet attained in the manufacture of Shingle Stains, being a scientific combination of linseed oil, coloring pigments, creosote oils and the necessary drying agents. It possesses great penetrative and preservative qualities and prolongs the life of the shingles by retarding decay, at the same time imparting an artistic finish.

We can supply SHINGLETINT in the following colors, which are indicated by numbers for convenience in ordering: No. 10 Buff, No. 20 Dark Red, No. 30 Light Green, No. 40 Brown, No. 50 Red, No. 60 Dark Green, No. 70 Light Gray, No. 80 Black, No. 90 Moss Green.

SHINGLETINT contains nothing of a poisonous nature, and will not spoil roof water when collected into a cistern for domestic purposes. It is customary and advisable, however, to allow the first few rains that occur after staining the shingles to run to waste so as to wash off the superfluous pigment which might otherwise impart an unpleasant taste to the water.

In SHINGLETINT the high water mark of quality in Shingle Stains is reached.

LACKLUSTRE.*

(TRADE MARK.)

T HIS is for producing the various dull effects on wood. The finish does not in any way resemble a rubbed varnish surface, but presents a dull and lustreless effect more like a wax finish.

A single operation produces the finish, which is adapted to both hard and soft woods, and the method of application is extremely simple, consisting merely of applying one coat with a soft brush and then wiping with a bunch of cotton waste or piece of cheese cloth.

We can supply LACKLUSTRE in the following colors: Green Flemish, Brown Flemish, Black Flemish, Golden, Mission, Antwerp, Filipino, Silver Gray, Light and Dark Weathered, Forest Green, and Bog.

We can also supply TRANSPARENT LACKLUSTRE if necessary but it must be distinctly understood that it should only be used over a stain, and has no value as a finish for applying to woods in the natural color.

If Water Stain is used in connection with Transparent Lacklustre, a thin coat of Shellac must fol-

---

*When we first introduced Lacklustre the process consisted of a coat of water stain followed by a thin coat of shellac and a coat of Lacklustre (which was transparent).

The one process Lacklustre described above supersedes the original process, and the use of the transparent Lacklustre is no longer necessary, the staining and finishing being done at a single operation.

low the Stain, as the Transparent Lacklustre causes the Water Stain to run unless a thin coat of Shellac is used over it as a fixative or binder.

The new style of wood finishing is as well adapted to soft woods as hard, and pine, poplar, cypress, and similar woods may be treated at very little expense, the finished result costing less than paint and being much more artistic in appearance.

Both cypress and yellow pine are susceptible to very artistic effects in dull finish, the broad markings of rift sawed yellow pine being especially effective.

OAK.

AMONG the many woods used for interior trim none have superseded oak in popularity. There are substantial reasons for this, as besides its great durability, oak has a very handsome grain, especially when quarter sawed, and this grain being susceptible of a greater variety of handsome effects by staining than any other wood used for interior finishing purposes, it is not to be wondered at that oak has the leading place among architectural woods.

The styles in oak finish change quite frequently, old "Finishes" becoming obsolete as new ones are introduced. Some styles meet with such favor that they become standard, but it is quite out of the question for them all to achieve enduring popularity.

We propose to make brief mention of such styles of oak finish as are in use at the present time, with such hints and directions for producing the various effects as are likely to be interesting and useful to the Architect, the Painter and Decorator.

GOLDEN OAK.

THIS is one of the most popular styles, and bids fair to become permanent. There is no universally accepted standard of color for it, and it has quite a wide latitude as to shade, varying according to locality and individual taste. Certain communities or manufacturing centers seem to establish a standard that has recognition in the markets controlled by or tributary to them, and outside of that other standards prevail, although they are mostly shades or modifications of rich brown or yellow, with the quarterings more or less prominent and of lighter color than the field.

SPECIFY AS FOLLOWS:

For An Egg Shell Gloss:—One coat of Berry Brothers' Golden Oak Water Stain, allow time to dry, then sandpaper lightly with fine sandpaper (to bring up the high lights) and apply a second coat of Stain diluted about one-half with water which will throw the grain into still higher relief, and so produce the effect of contrast that constitutes one of the features of Golden Oak. Follow with a light coat of thin Shellac, sand lightly with fine sandpaper, and fill with Berry Brothers' Paste Filler colored to match the stain, then give a coat of Orange Shellac, sand lightly and finish with two or three coats of Berry Brothers' Luxeberry Wood Finish (White or Light); rub first coats with hair cloth or curled hair, and the last coat with pulverized pumice stone and crude oil or raw linseed oil.

For a Dull Finish:—Specify that the last coat be rubbed with pulverized pumice stone and water, instead of oil.

For a Polished Finish:—Specify that the last coat be rubbed first with pulverized pumice stone and water, and then with pulverized rotten stone and water, and for a piano finish specify a further rubbing with Berry Brothers' Furniture Polish, used with a little pulverized rotten stone, applied with a piece of soft felt or flannel.

If a rubbed finish is not desired, omit the specifications for rubbing the last coat.

NOTES.

THE above directions are for what is known as dark Golden Oak; light Golden Oak is produced in precisely the same manner, except that the Stain is not so dark, the filler being the same in either case.

Use Berry Brothers' Light Paste Filler and bring to the right shade by mixing in Burnt Umber and Venetian red until the desired color is obtained. The right proportion is about 12 ozs. burnt umber and 4 ozs. Venetian red to 20 lbs. of light paste filler.

GOLDEN OAK.

ANOTHER WAY.

FILL with a coat of Berry Brothers' Golden Oak Paste Filler, and follow with a coat of Berry Brothers' Golden Oak Granitum and a coat of Shellac.

Sandpaper and finish with two or three coats of Berry Brothers' Luxeberry Wood Finish (White or Light), in the same manner as directed above.

This method is quicker than some and produces a very handsome finish. It may not suit everybody's ideas as to what Golden Oak should be, but it is artistic and we shall be pleased to send samples of finished wood showing what it looks like.

ENGLISH OAK, SUMATRA BROWN, DUTCH BROWN.

SPECIFY AS FOLLOWS:

FOR AN EGG SHELL GLOSS:—One coat of Berry Brothers' Water Stain, English Oak, Sumatra Brown or Dutch Brown, as the case may be, allow time to dry, sandpaper lightly with fine sandpaper (to bring up the high lights) and apply a second coat of stain diluted about one-half with water. Follow with a light coat of thin Shellac, sand lightly with fine sandpaper, and fill with Berry Brothers' Dark Paste Filler, then give a coat of Orange Shellac, sand lightly again, and finish with two or three coats of Berry Brothers' Luxeberry Wood Finish (White or Light) ; rub first coats with hair cloth or curled hair, and the last coat with pulverized pumice stone and crude oil or raw linseed oil.

For a Dull Finish:—Specify that the last coat be rubbed with pulverized pumice stone and water instead of oil.

For a Polished Finish:—Specify that the last coat be rubbed first with pulverized pumice stone and water and then with pulverized rotten stone and water, and for a piano finish specify a further rubbing with Berry Brothers' Furniture Polish, used with a little pulverized rotten stone, applied with a piece of soft felt or flannel.

If a rubbed finish is not desired, omit the specifications for rubbing the last coat.

NOTES.

THE paste filler for the above is prepared in the same manner as for Golden Oak, the same pigments being used, and practically the same proportions (12 ozs. burnt umber and 4 ozs. Venetian red to 20 lbs. light paste filler), but varied slightly according to the desired result.

The English Oak comes pretty closely in color to the genuine wood, which is a dark brown.

Sumatra Brown has a noticeable tint of red in it, giving the finish a rich, warm color, the marking of the grain also being tinged with a reddish brown instead of standing out light as they do on the English Oak.

Dutch Brown is a still warmer color, owing to a trifle more Venetian Red being used in the filler. The grain of the wood shows up very handsomely but is strongly tinged with the prevailing color of the finish.

It is the same with the three above named Finishes as with others of the Brown and Yellow groups; there is no recognized and fixed standard of color, so that it is impossible to give exact and definite descriptions.

BROWN FLEMISH.

This is a rich, deep brown, somewhat resembling the English Oak, but darker in tone.

SPECIFY AS FOLLOWS:

FOR AN EGG SHELL GLOSS:—One coat Berry Brothers' Brown Flemish Water Stain. When dry, sand lightly with fine sandpaper and apply a second coat of Stain reduced about one-half with water. Follow with a light coat of thin Shellac, sand lightly with fine sandpaper, and fill with Berry Brothers' light paste filler, tinted to the right shade with Vandyke Brown. Sand lightly with 00 sandpaper and then give a coat of Orange Shellac, sand lightly again and follow with two or three coats of Berry Brothers' Luxeberry Wood Finish (White or Light); rub first coats with hair cloth or curled hair, and the last coat with pulverized pumice stone and crude oil or raw linseed oil.

For a Dull Finish:—Specify that the last coat be rubbed with pulverized pumice stone and water instead of oil.

For a Polished Finish:—Specify that the last coat be rubbed first with pulverized pumice stone and water, and then with pulverized rotten stone and water, and for a piano finish specify a further rubbing with Berry Brothers' Furniture Polish, used with a little pulverized rotten stone, applied with a piece of soft felt or flannel.

If a rubbed finish is not desired, omit the specifications for rubbing the last coat.

GREEN FLEMISH.

THIS is really an old finish under a new name; when first introduced some years ago it was known as water oak, and had quite a following; it gradually died out, however, and has more recently been revived under the name of "Green Flemish."

While very sombre in tone, this is a very handsome finish, the general effect being black, but relieved by high lights of a greenish gray.

SPECIFY AS FOLLOWS:

FOR AN EGG SHELL GLOSS:—One coat of Berry Brothers' Green Flemish Water Stain, when dry, sand lightly with fine sandpaper, and apply a second coat of the stain diluted about one-half with water. Follow with a light coat of thin Shellac, sand lightly and fill with black paste filler. Sand lightly again with 00 sandpaper, and then give a coat of Orange Shellac, sandpaper, and follow with two or three coats of Berry Brothers' Luxeberry Wood Finish (White or Light); rub first coats with hair cloth, or curled hair, and the last coat with pulverized pumice stone and crude oil or raw linseed oil.

FOR A DULL FINISH:—Specify that the last coat be rubbed with pulverized pumice stone and water instead of oil.

For a Polished Finish:—Specify that the last coat be rubbed first with pulverized pumice stone and water and then with pulverized rotten stone and water, and for a piano finish specify a further rubbing with Berry Brothers' Furniture Polish, used with a little pulverized rotten stone, applied with a piece of soft felt or flannel.

If a rubbed finish is not desired, omit the specifications for rubbing the last coat.

BLACK FLEMISH.

This, as its name indicates, is a black effect unrelieved by any other shade. The markings of quartered oak can be faintly seen but the general effect is a solid black.

SPECIFY AS FOLLOWS:

For an Egg Shell Gloss: One coat of Berry Brothers Black Flemish Water Stain, when dry, sand lightly with fine sandpaper and fill with black paste filler. Sand lightly again with 00 sandpaper, and then give a coat of Orange Shellac, sandpaper, and follow with two or three coats of Berry Brothers' Luxeberry Wood Finish (White or Light); rub first coats with hair cloth or curled hair, and the last coat with pulverized pumice stone and crude oil or raw linseed oil.

FOR A DULL FINISH:—Specify that the last coat be rubbed with pulverized pumice stone and water instead of oil.

FOR A POLISHED FINISH:—Specify that the last coat be rubbed first with pulverized pumice stone and water and then with pulverized rotten stone and water, and for a piano finish specify a further rubbing with Berry Brothers' Furniture Polish, used with a little pulverized rotten stone, applied with a piece of soft felt or flannel.

If a rubbed finish is not desired, omit the specifications for rubbing the last coat.

NOTES.

THE term Flemish is very indefinite, as the finishes known by this name differ widely in appearance; finishers being by no means unanimous as to its color, which varies from dead black through a number of shades or sub-tints of gray, green, brown and blue, the background in all cases being black or very dark.

The two styles of Flemish described above have the widest popularity and will be found to fill most demands.

For the Brown Flemish finish use Berry Brothers' Light Paste Filler colored with Vandyke Brown and Venetian Red, in the proportion of 12 ozs. Vandyke Brown and 4 ozs. Venetian Red to 20 lbs. Light Paste Filler. For the Green Flemish use Berry Brothers' Light Paste Filler colored with drop black or dry lamp black.

OX BLOOD.

T HIS is a comparatively new style of finish, the name being indicative of its color, which is a bright red.

The quarterings show up very nicely and the general effect is bright and showy.

SPECIFY AS FOLLOWS:

FOR AN EGG SHELL GLOSS:—One coat of Berry Brothers' Ox Blood Water Stain; when dry, sand lightly with fine sandpaper and then apply a second coat of Stain reduced about one-half with water. Follow with a light coat of thin Shellac, sand lightly, and fill with light paste filler colored to match the Stain.

When dry, sand lightly with 00 sandpaper and follow with a coat of orange Shellac. Give another light sanding and apply two or three coats of Berry Brothers' Luxeberry Wood Finish (White or Light) rub first coats with hair cloth or curled hair, and the last coat with pulverized pumice stone and crude oil or raw linseed oil.

FOR A DULL FINISH:—Specify that the last coat be rubbed with pulverized pumice stone and water, instead of oil.

FOR A POLISHED FINISH:—Specify that the last coat be rubbed first with pulverized pumice stone and water, and then with pulverized rotten stone and water, and for a piano finish specify a further rubbing with Berry Brothers' Furniture Polish, used with a little pulverized rotten stone, applied with a piece of soft felt or flannel.

If a rubbed finish is not desired, omit the specifications for rubbing the last coat.

NOTES.

The Filler for the above finish is prepared by adding 12 ozs. dry Rose Lake to 20 lbs. of Berry Brothers' Light Paste Filler.

FOREST GREEN.

———

THIS is a very handsome finish, although a decided novelty in the way of oak finishing. It is a very soft color, being a shade of yellow green, somewhat resembling the first leaves of spring.

SPECIFY AS FOLLOWS:

FOR AN EGG SHELL GLOSS:—One coat Berry Brothers' Forest Green Water Stain. When dry, sand lightly with fine sandpaper and then apply a coat of Forest Green Water Stain reduced about one-half with water. Follow with a light coat of thin Shellac, sand lightly and fill with light paste filler colored with chrome green in the proportion of one lb. to 20 lbs. of Berry Brothers' Light Paste Filler. When dry, sand lightly with 00 sandpaper and follow with a coat of Orange Shellac. Give another light sanding and apply two or three coats of Berry Brothers' Luxeberry Wood Finish (White or Light); rub first coats with hair cloth or curled hair, and the last coat with pulverized pumice stone and crude oil or raw linseed oil.

FOR A DULL FINISH:—Specify that the last coat be rubbed with pulverized pumice stone and water instead of oil.

FOR A POLISHED FINISH:—Specify that the last coat be rubbed first with pulverized pumice stone and water, and then with pulverized rotten stone and water, and for a piano finish specify a further rubbing with Berry Brothers' Furniture Polish, used with a little pulverized rotten stone, applied with a piece of soft felt or flannel.

If a rubbed finish is not desired, omit the specifications for rubbing the last coat.

MALACHITE.

THIS is also a green finish, but of a different shade to Forest Green. It lacks the yellow quality, and has a somewhat brighter appearance, the green having a bluish cast.

SPECIFY AS FOLLOWS:

FOR AN EGG SHELL GLOSS:—One coat of Berry Brothers' Malachite Water Stain; when dry, sand lightly with a fine sandpaper and then apply a second coat of stain reduced about one-half with water. Follow with a light coat of thin Shellac, sand lightly and fill with Berry Brothers' Black paste filler. When dry, sand lightly with 00 sandpaper and follow with a coat of Orange Shellac, sand lightly again, and apply two or three coats of Berry Brothers' Luxeberry Wood Finish (White or Light); rub first coats with hair cloth or curled hair, and the last coat with pulverized pumice stone and crude oil or raw linseed oil.

For a Dull Finish:—Specify that the last coat be rubbed with pulverized pumice stone and water instead of oil.

For a Polished Finish:—Specify that the last coat be rubbed first with pulverized pumice stone and water, and then with pulverized rotten stone and water, and for a piano finish specify a further rubbing with Berry Brothers' Furniture Polish, used with a little pulverized rotten stone, applied with a piece of soft felt or flannel.

If a rubbed finish is not desired, omit the specifications for rubbing the last coat.

FILIPINO.

A NEW shade, the general tone of which is very dark, the field black and the marking of the grain a sort of dark mossy green.

FOR AN EGG SHELL GLOSS:—One coat of Berry Brothers' Filipino Water Stain; when dry, sand lightly with fine sandpaper, and apply a second coat of the stain diluted about one-half with water. Follow with a light coat of thin Shellac, sand lightly and fill with black paste filler. Sand lightly again with .00 sand-paper, and then give a coat of Orange Shellac; sand-paper, and follow with two or three coats of Berry Brothers' Luxeberry Wood Finish (White or Light); rub first coats with hair cloth or curled hair, and the last coat with pulverized pumice stone and crude oil or raw linseed oil.

FOR A DULL FINISH:—Specify that the last coat be rubbed with pulverized pumice stone and water instead of oil.

FOR A POLISHED FINISH:—Specify that the last coat be rubbed first with pulverized pumice stone and water, and then with pulverized rotten stone and water, and for a piano finish specify a further rubbing with Berry Brothers' Furniture Polish used with a little pulverized rotten stone, applied with a piece of soft felt or flannel.

If a rubbed finish is not desired, omit the specifications for rubbing the last coat.

AUSTRIAN.

THIS is a shade of grayish brown with the grain faintly showing through in nearly the same color.

SPECIFY AS FOLLOWS:

One coat of Berry Brothers' Austrian Oak Stain, sand lightly with fine sandpaper and then apply a coat of black paste filler, followed by a light coat of thin White Shellac in which a little black has been dissolved, and a coat of Transparent "Lacklustre."

NOTES.

IT is important to follow explicitly our directions for using a *thin* shellac coat, as it is merely intended in this case to act as a binder for the filler coat, and should dry flat so as not to spoil the dull effect of a finish.

This finish has met with some favor in the gloss effect, and although the color tone is not exactly the same as described on preceding page, it is quite a pleasing shade and has some popularity.

SPECIFY AS FOLLOWS:

For an Egg Shell Gloss:—One coat of Berry Brother's Austrian Oak Stain; when dry sand lightly with fine sandpaper and fill with Black Paste Filler. Follow with a coat of White Shellac, sand lightly with 00 Sandpaper and follow with two or three coats of Berry Brothers' Luxeberry Wood Finish (White or Light); rub first coats with hair cloth or curled hair, and the last coat with pulverized pumice stone and crude oil or raw linseed oil.

For a Dull Finish:—Specify that the last coat be rubbed with pulverized pumice stone and water, instead of oil.

For a Polished Finish:—Specify that the last coat be rubbed first with pulverized pumice stone and water and then with pulverized rotten stone and water, and for a piano finish specify a further rubbing with Berry Brothers' Furniture Polish, used with a little pulverized rotten stone, applied with a piece of soft felt or flannel.

If a rubbed finish is not desired, omit the specifications for rubbing the last coat.

ROTTERDAM.

T HIS is a very dark finish, something on the Black
Flemish order with the grain showing through
a sort of yellowish white like discolored white pine.
The desired effect demands an absolutely dull surface
and is never seen in varnish or gloss finish.

SPECIFY AS FOLLOWS:

One coat of Berry Brothers' Rotterdam Water
Stain, sand lightly with fine sandpaper and apply
a light coat of thin Shellac and a coat of black paste
filler in the order named, followed by a coat of
Transparent "Lacklustre."

WEATHERED OAK.

There is no universally accepted standard of color
for the so-called "Weathered" effect, but the shades
we describe have the widest popularity and are
what we always furnish when Weathered Oak Stain
is ordered.

The Light Weathered effect is a composite color
in appearance—yellow, brown and green all blend-
ing in the general color tone,—the open grain of
the wood being black, and the quarterings showing

up a trifle lighter than the field. The Dark Weathered effect has the same general characteristics as the Light, but the color tone is deeper.

NOTES.

While it is true that the Weathered Oak finish is generally seen as one of the dull effects, it is sometimes varnished, and when this is desired,

SPECIFY AS FOLLOWS:

FOR AN EGG SHELL GLOSS:—One coat of Berry Brothers' Light or Dark Weathered Oak Stain; dry, sand lightly with fine sandpaper, and apply a second coat of the stain diluted about one-half with water. Follow with a light coat of thin Shellac, sand lightly and fill with black paste filler. Sand lightly again with 00 sandpaper, and then give a coat of Orange Shellac, sandpaper, and follow with two or three coats of Berry Brothers' Luxeberry Wood Finish (White or Light); rub first coats with hair cloth or curled hair and the last coat with pulverized pumice stone and crude oil or raw linseed oil.

FOR A DULL FINISH:—Specify that the last coat be rubbed with pulverized pumice stone and water, instead of oil.

For a Polished Finish:—Specify that the last coat be rubbed first with pulverized pumice stone and water and then with pulverized rotten stone and water, and for a *piano finish* specify a further rubbing with Berry· Brothers' Furniture Polish, used with a little pulverized rotten stone, applied with a piece of soft felt or flannel.

If a rubbed finish is not desired, omit the specifications for rubbing the last coat.

SILVER GRAY.

THIS belongs in reality to the "Weathered" Oak group, but owing to its distinctive style it has become known as Silver Gray.

Its appearance is fairly described by the name, which is a light gray with the quarterings showing through in the same general color tone, but a trifle on the yellow order.

SPECIFY AS FOLLOWS:

For an Egg Shell Gloss:—One coat of Berry Brothers' Silver Gray Water Stain; when dry, sand lightly with fine sandpaper, and follow with a light coat of thin Shellac, sand lightly and fill with light paste filler to which a little flake white has been added.

Sand lightly with 00 sandpaper and then give a coat of White Shellac, sandpaper, and follow with two or three coats of Berry Brothers' Luxeberry Wood Finish (White or Light) ; rub first coats with hair cloth or curled hair, and the last coat with pulverized pumice stone and crude oil or raw linseed oil.

For a Dull Finish :—Specify that the last coat be rubbed with pulverized pumice stone and water instead of oil.

For a Polished Finish :—Specify that the last coat be rubbed first with pulverized pumice stone and water, and then with pulverized rotten stone and water, and for a piano finish specify a further rubbing with Berry Brothers' Furniture Polish, used with a little pulverized rotten stone, applied with a piece of soft felt or flannel.

If a rubbed finish is not desired, omit the specifications for rubbing the last coat.

NOTES.

Oak, Ash, Chestnut and other open-grained woods present an artistic appearance in the Silver Gray effect, and Yellow Pine and Cypress also look well finished this way, especially if the woods have nice, broad markings. Bird's eye maple looks particularly handsome in the Silver Gray effect.

ANTIQUE.

PERHAPS no style of Oak Finish has a wider latitude as to color than the so-called "Antique," and there is no fixed standard for it otherwise than it is brown or some modification of it, and the only solution of the point is for the finisher to defer to the wishes of his patron. "Antique" Oak may be stained or not as may be desired, and a popular shade of "Antique" may be had by simply filling the grain of the wood with dark or Antique paste filler, following with a coat of Shellac, and finishing in the regular way.

If other effects are wanted, the wood should be stained and treated in the same manner as for Golden, English and other styles of oak.

SPECIFY AS FOLLOWS:

FOR AN EGG SHELL GLOSS:—One coat of Berry Brothers' Antique Water Stain; when dry, sand lightly with fine sandpaper, and then apply a second coat Antique Oak Stain diluted about one-half with water. Follow with a light coat of thin Shellac, sand lightly and fill with light paste filler colored to the desired shade with Vandyke Brown and Venetian Red in the proportion of 12 ozs. Vandyke Brown and 4 ozs. Venetian Red to 20 lbs. Berry Brothers' Light Paste Filler. When dry, sand lightly with 00 sandpaper and follow with a coat of Orange Shellac, sand lightly again and apply two or three coats of Berry Brothers' Luxeberry Wood Finish (White or Light); rub first coats with hair cloth or curled hair, and the last coat with pulverized pumice stone and crude oil or raw linseed oil.

For a Dull Finish:—Specify that the last coat be rubbed with pulverized pumice stone and water instead of oil.

For a Polished Finish.—Specify that the last coat be rubbed first with pulverized pumice stone and water and then with pulverized rotten stone and water, and for a piano finish specify a further rubbing with Berry Brothers' Furniture Polish, used with a little pulverized rotten stone, applied with a piece of soft felt or flannel.

If a rubbed finish is not desired, omit the specifications for rubbing the last coat.

MISSION OAK.

SPECIFY AS FOLLOWS:

FOR AN EGG SHELL GLOSS:—One coat of Berry Brothers' Mission Oak Water Stain; when dry, sand with fine sandpaper and apply a second coat of Stain diluted about one-half with water. Follow with a light coat of thin Shellac, sand lightly and fill with Berry Brothers' light paste filler, colored to match the stain. When dry, sand lightly with 00 sandpaper, and give a coat of Orange Shellac. Sand lightly again and follow with two or three coats of Berry Brothers' Luxeberrry Wood Finish (White or Light); rub first coats with haircloth or curled hair, and the last coat with pulverized pumice stone and crude oil or raw linseed oil.

FOR A POLISHED FINISH:—Specify that the last coat be rubbed first with pulverized pumice stone and water and then with pulverized rotten stone and water, and for a piano finish specify a further rubbing with Berry Brothers' Furniture Polish, used with a little pulverized rotten stone, applied with a piece of soft felt or flannel.

If a rubbed finish is not desired, omit the specifications for rubbing the last coat.

NOTES.

FOR the above finish use Berry Brothers' Light Paste Filler colored with Umber and Venetian Red; 12 ounces of Umber and 4 ounces of Venetian Red to 20 pounds of filler will give about the shade required.

The color of "Mission Oak" is a shade between the "English" and "Dark Golden" finishes, the quartering being in less pronounced contrast to the field than in either the "Dark Golden" or "English" finishes.

CATHEDRAL OAK.

SPECIFY AS FOLLOWS:

FOR AN EGG SHELL GLOSS:—One coat of Berry Brothers' Cathedral Oak Water Stain; when dry, sand with fine sandpaper, and apply a second coat of the stain diluted about one-half with water. Follow with a thin coat of Shellac, sand lightly and fill with Berry Brothers' paste filler, colored to match the stain. When dry, sand lightly with 00 sandpaper and apply a coat of Orange Shellac. Sand lightly again and follow with two or three coats of Berry Brothers'

Luxeberry Wood Finish (White or Light); rub first coats with hair cloth or curled hair, and the last coat with pulverized pumice stone and crude oil or raw linseed oil.

FOR A DULL FINISH:—Specify that the last coat be rubbed with pulverized pumice stone and water, instead of oil.

FOR A POLISHED FINISH:—Specify that the last coat be rubbed first with pulverized pumice stone and water and then with pulverized rotten stone and water, and for a piano finish specify a further rubbing with Berry Brothers' Furniture Polish, used with a little pulverized rotten stone, applied with a piece of soft felt or flannel.

If a rubbed finish is not desired, omit the specifications for rubbing the last coat.

NOTES.

THE color tone of this style of finish is of the same order as "Brown Flemish," the field being as dark, but the general effect a trifle less sombre by reason of the quarterings being lighter and showing up in higher relief.

For this finish use Berry Brothers' Light Paste Filler colored with Vandyke Brown in the proportion of 1 lb. to 20 lbs. filler.

BOG OAK.

THIS is quite a handsome style of finish, although very dark in tone, the field being black and the quarterings showing through in a shade of yellowish green.

SPECIFY AS FOLLOWS:

FOR AN EGG SHELL GLOSS:—One coat of Berry Brothers' Bog Oak Water Stain; allow time to dry; sand with fine sandpaper and then apply a second coat of Stain diluted about one-half with water. Follow with a light coat of thin Shellac, sand lightly and fill with black paste filler; when dry, sand lightly with 00 sandpaper and follow with a coat of Orange Shellac, sand again and apply two or three coats of Berry Brothers' Luxeberry Wood Finish (White or Light); rub first coats with hair cloth or curled hair, and the last coat with pulverized pumice stone and crude oil or raw linseed oil.

For a Dull Finish:—Specify that the last coat be rubbed with pulverized pumice stone and water, instead of oil.

For a Polished Finish:—Specify that the last coat be rubbed first with pulverized pumice stone and water and then with pulverized rotten stone and water, and for a piano finish specify a further rubbing with Berry Brothers' Furniture Polish, used with a little pulverized rotten stone, applied with a piece of soft felt or flannel.

If a rubbed finish is not desired, omit the specifications for rubbing the last coat.

ANTWERP OAK.

When the dull effect is wanted,

SPECIFY AS FOLLOWS:

One coat of Berry Brothers' Antwerp Lacklustre applied with a soft brush and wiped off with a bunch of cotton waste or piece of cheese cloth.

When a gloss finish is wanted,

SPECIFY AS FOLLOWS:

FOR AN EGG SHELL GLOSS:—One coat of Berry Brothers' Antwerp Water Stain. When dry, sand lightly with fine sandpaper and apply a second coat of Stain, reduced about one-half with water. Follow with a light coat of thin Shellac, sand lightly with fine sandpaper and fill with Berry Brothers' Black Paste Filler. Sand lightly with 00 sandpaper, and then give a coat of Orange Shellac, sand lightly again and follow with two or three coats of Berry Brothers' Luxeberry Wood Finish (White or Light); rub first coats with hair cloth or curled hair, and the last coat with pulverized pumice stone and crude oil or raw linseed oil.

FOR A DULL FINISH:—Specify that the last coat be rubbed with pulverized pumice stone and water instead of oil.

FOR A POLISHED FINISH:—Specify that the last coat be rubbed first with pulverized pumice stone and water, and then with pulverized rotten stone and water and for a piano finish specify a further rubbing with Berry Brothers' Furniture Polish, used with a little pulverized rotten stone, applied with a piece of soft felt or flannel.

If a rubbed finish is not desired, omit the specifications for the last coat.

NOTES.

THIS was originally one of the dull finishes and until recently was never varnished, but it is now gradually being adopted as one of the gloss finishes. The general color tone is very dark brown, the black filler emphasizing the sombre effect, which however, is relieved somewhat by the markings which show through in a lighter brown than the prevailing shade.

ASH, CHESTNUT.

THESE are open grained woods and require filling. When it is desired to finish in the natural color without staining,

SPECIFY AS FOLLOWS:

FOR AN EGG SHELL GLOSS:—One coat of Berry Brothers' Light Paste Filler, followed by one coat of

White Shellac sandpapered to a smooth surface, and two or three coats of Berry Brothers' Luxeberrry Wood Finish (White or Light); rub first coats with hair cloth or curled hair, and the last coat with pulverized pumice stone and crude oil or raw linseed oil.

FOR A DULL FINISH:—Specify that the last coat be rubbed with pulverized pumice stone and water, instead of oil.

FOR A POLISHED FINISH:—Specify that the last coat be rubbed first with pulverized pumice stone and water and then with pulverized rotten stone and water, and for a *piano finish* specify a further rubbing with Berry Brothers' Furniture Polish, used with a little pulverized rotten stone, applied with a piece of soft felt or flannel.

If a rubbed finish is not desired, omit the specifications for rubbing the last coat.

NOTES.

BOTH Ash and Chestnut are susceptible of rich and varied effects by staining, the large, open grain and broad markings, especially on the chestnut, lending themselves to very artistic treatment. Both these woods can be handled by the finisher in precisely the same manner as oak, using the same stains and employing the same methods as described in the preceding pages on Oak.

MAHOGANY.

T HIS belongs to the open grained woods and requires filling.

SPECIFY AS FOLLOWS:

FOR AN EGG SHELL GLOSS:—One coat of Berry Brothers' Paste Filler to match the color of the wood, followed by a coat of Orange Shellac sandpapered to a smooth surface, and two or three coats of Berry Brothers' Luxeberry Wood Finish (White or Light); rub first coats with hair cloth or curled hair, and the last coat with pulverized pumice stone and crude oil or raw linseed oil.

FOR A DULL FINISH:—Specify that the last coat be rubbed with pulverized pumice stone and water, instead of oil.

FOR A POLISHED FINISH:—Specify that the last coat be rubbed first with pulverized pumice stone and water and then with pulverized rotten stone and water, and for a *piano finish* specify a further rubbing with Berry Brothers' Furniture Polish, used with a little pulverized rotten stone, applied with a piece of soft felt or flannel.

If a rubbed finish is not desired, omit the specifications for rubbing the last coat.

NOTES.

IF it is required to deepen the natural color of Mahogany, it can be done by using a light filler darkened with burnt sienna to the desired tint.

If "antique" or dark Mahogany is required, precede the filling by staining the wood with a solution of bi-chromate of potash and water, or a coat of Berry Brothers' Mahogany Stain.

Much of the so-called Mahogany in present use is in reality Baywood or American Mahogany, as it is called. This wood is very much lighter in color than true Mahogany and is rather cold and insipid in tone when finished in the natural color.

PRIMA VERA OR WHITE MAHOGANY.

T HIS wood is open grained and must be filled. It is invariably finished in the natural color, as staining would mar its delicate shade and markings.

SPECIFY AS FOLLOWS:

FOR AN EGG SHELL GLOSS:—One coat of Berry Brothers' Light Paste Filler, followed by one coat of White Shellac sandpapered to a smooth surface and two or three coats of Berry Brothers' Luxeberry Wood Finish (White); rub first coats with hair cloth or curled hair, and the last coat with pulverized pumice stone and crude oil or raw linseed oil.

FOR A DULL FINISH:—Specify that the last coat be rubbed with pulverized pumice stone and water, instead of oil.

FOR A POLISHED FINISH:—Specify that the last coat be rubbed first with pulverized pumice stone and water and then with pulverized rotten stone and water, and for a *piano finish* specify a further rubbing with Berry Brothers' Furniture Polish, used with a little pulverized rotten stone, applied with a piece of soft felt or flannel.

If a rubbed finish is not desired, omit the specifications for rubbing the last coat.

CHERRY.

THIS is a close grained wood and requires no filling. When it is desired to finish in the natural color,

SPECIFY AS FOLLOWS:

FOR AN EGG SHELL GLOSS:—One coat of Orange Shellac sandpapered to a smooth surface, followed by two or three coats of Berry Brothers' Luxeberry Wood Finish (White or Light); rub first coats with hair cloth or curled hair, and the last coat with pulverized pumice stone and crude oil or raw linseed oil.

FOR A DULL FINISH:—Specify that the last coat be rubbed with pulverized pumice stone and water, instead of oil.

FOR A POLISHED FINISH:—Specify that the last coat be rubbed first with pulverized pumice stone and water and then with pulverized rotten stone and water, and for a *piano finish* specify a further rubbing with Berry Brothers' Furniture Polish, used with a little pulverized rotten stone, applied with a piece of soft felt or flannel.

If a rubbed finish is not desired, omit the specifications for rubbing the last coat.

NOTES.

A LTHOUGH Cherry is a very beautiful wood in its natural state, some tastes may prefer a deeper color, which necessitates the staining of the wood to the desired shade. In such cases precede the Shellac coat with a coat of Berry Brothers' Stain, Cherry or Mahogany, as may be desired.

If the wood is required to be finished up as light as possible, specify White Shellac instead of Orange Shellac and omit staining.

SYCAMORE.

T HIS wood is usually quarter sawed for finishing purposes; it is almost invariably finished in the natural color, and being close grained, needs no filler.

SPECIFY AS FOLLOWS:

FOR AN EGG SHELL GLOSS:—One coat of Shellac (White Shellac if the natural color of the wood is to be preserved, or Orange Shellac if the wood is desired to be a little darker in tone); sandpaper to a smooth surface and follow with two or three coats of Berry Brothers' Luxeberry Wood Finish (White or Light) specify Luxeberry Wood Finish white, if the natural color of the wood is to be retained; rub first coats with hair cloth or curled hair, and the last coat with pulverized pumice stone and crude oil or raw linseed oil.

FOR A DULL FINISH:—Specify that the last coat be rubbed with pulverized pumice stone and water, instead of oil.

FOR A POLISHED FINISH:—Specify that the last coat be rubbed first with pulverized pumice stone and water and then with pulverized rotten stone and water, and for a *piano finish* specify a further rubbing with Berry Brothers' Furniture Polish used with a little pulverized rotten stone, applied with a piece of soft felt or flannel.

If a rubbed finish is not desired, omit the specifications for rubbing the last coat.

BEECH.

———

THIS wood, while not extensively used hitherto in architectural work, is now being brought forward for interior trim, and makes a very handsome appearance when properly treated, especially when quarter sawed.

It is close grained and needs no filling.

SPECIFY AS FOLLOWS:

FOR AN EGG SHELL GLOSS:—One coat of White Shellac sandpapered to a smooth surface, followed by two or three coats of Berry Brothers' Luxeberry Wood Finish (White or Light); rub first coats with hair cloth or curled hair and the last coat with pulverized pumice stone and crude oil or raw linseed oil.

FOR A DULL FINISH:—Specify that the last coat be rubbed with pulverized pumice stone and water, and then with pulverized rotten stone and water, and for a piano finish specify a further rubbing with Berry

Brothers' Furniture Polish, used with a little pulverized rotten stone, applied with a piece of soft felt or flannel.

If a rubbed finish is not desired, omit the specifications for rubbing the last coat.

NOTES.

THE above specifications provide for finishing the wood in the natural color, but if desired, handsome effects can be produced by staining.

The wood takes Mahogany and Walnut Stains very well, and an excellent "Cherry" can be made with the Red Beech.

When this wood is stained specify Orange Shellac and precede the shellac coat with a coat of Berry Brothers' Stain, "Mahogany," "Cherry," "Walnut" or otherwise, as may be preferred.

MAPLE.

———

THIS is close grained and does not require filling. For finishing in the natural color,

SPECIFY AS FOLLOWS:

FOR AN EGG SHELL GLOSS:—One coat of White Shellac sandpapered to a smooth surface, followed by two or three coats of Berry Brothers' Luxeberry Wood Finish (White); rub first coats with hair cloth or curled hair, and the last coat with pulverized pumice stone and crude oil or raw linseed oil.

For a Dull Finish:—Specify that the last coat be rubbed with pulverized pumice stone and water, instead of oil.

For a Polished Finish:—Specify that the last coat be rubbed first with pulverized pumice stone and water and then with pulverized rotten stone and water, and for a *piano finish* specify a further rubbing with Berry Brothers' Furniture Polish, used with a little pulverized rotten stone, applied with a piece of soft felt or flannel.

If a rubbed finish is not desired, omit the specifications for rubbing the last coat.

NOTES.

MAPLE is susceptible of very rich effects in Cherry and Mahogany by staining. If stained, specify Orange Shellac, and precede the Shellac coat with a coat of Berry Brothers' Stain, "Cherry" or "Mahogany," or otherwise as may be desired.

BIRCH.

THIS is a close grained wood and needs no filling. For finishing in the natural color,

SPECIFY AS FOLLOWS:

FOR AN EGG SHELL GLOSS:—One coat of White Shellac sandpapered to a smooth surface, followed by two or three coats of Berry Brothers' Luxeberry Wood Finish (White or Light); rub first coats with hair cloth or curled hair, and the last coat with pulverized pumice stone and crude oil or raw linseed oil.

FOR A DULL FINISH:—Specify that the last coat be rubbed with pulverized pumice stone and water, instead of oil.

FOR A POLISHED FINISH:—Specify that the last coat be rubbed first with pulverized pumice stone and water and then with pulverized rotten stone and water, and for a *piano finish* specify a further rubbing with Berry Brothers' Furniture Polish, used with a little pulverized rotten stone, applied with a piece of soft felt or flannel.

If a rubbed finish is not desired, omit the specifications for rubbing the last coat.

NOTES.

I F a deeper tone is required specify Orange Shellac instead of White Shellac.

Birch also takes stain very nicely if the right kind is used. Cherry and Mahogany look particularly well on Birch. If stained, specify Orange Shellac, and precede the Shellac coat with a coat of Berry Brothers' Stain, "Cherry," "Mahogany," or otherwise, as may be desired.

WALNUT, BUTTERNUT.

B OTH of the above are open grained woods and require filling.

SPECIFY AS FOLLOWS:

FOR AN EGG SHELL GLOSS:—One coat of Berry Brothers' Paste Filler to match the color of the wood, followed by a coat of Orange Shellac sandpapered to a smooth surface, and two or three coats of Berry Brothers' Luxeberry Wood Finish (White or Light); rub first coats with hair cloth or curled hair, and the last coat with pulverized pumice stone and crude oil or raw linseed oil.

FOR A DULL FINISH:—Specify that the last coat be rubbed with pulverized pumice stone and water, instead of oil.

FOR A POLISHED FINISH:—Specify that the last coat be rubbed first with pulverized pumice stone and water and then with pulverized rotten stone and water, and for a *piano finish* specify a further rubbing with Berry Brothers' Furniture Polish, used with a little pulverized rotten stone, applied with a piece of soft felt or flannel.

If a rubbed finish is not desired, omit the specifications for rubbing the last coat.

GUM WOOD.

THIS is close grained and needs no filling.

SPECIFY AS FOLLOWS:

FOR AN EGG SHELL GLOSS:—One coat of Orange Shellac sandpapered to a smooth surface, followed by two or three coats of Berry Brothers' Luxeberry Wood Finish (White or Light); rub first coats with hair cloth or curled hair, and the last coat with pulverized pumice stone and crude oil or raw linseed oil.

FOR A DULL FINISH:—Specify that the last coat be rubbed with pulverized pumice stone and water, instead of oil.

FOR A POLISHED FINISH:—Specify that the last coat be rubbed first with pulverized pumice stone and water and then with pulverized rotten stone and water, and for a *piano finish* specify a further rubbing with Berry Brothers' Furniture Polish, used with a little pulverized rotten stone, applied with a piece of soft felt or flannel.

If a rubbed finish is not desired, omit the specifications for rubbing the last coat.

NOTES.

THE above specifications provide for finishing the wood in its natural color.

Gum Wood can also be stained quite successfully and looks very handsome when properly done. Mahogany and Cherry are the most popular stains for this wood. If stained, specify Orange Shellac, and precede the Shellac coat with a coat of Berry Brothers' Stain, "Mahogany," "Cherry," or otherwise, as may be preferred.

REDWOOD, CEDAR.

T HESE are close grained woods and need no filling.

SPECIFY AS FOLLOWS:

FOR AN EGG SHELL GLOSS:—One coat of Orange Shellac sandpapered to a smooth surface, followed by two or three coats of Berry Brothers' Luxeberry Wood Finish (White or Light); rub first coats with hair cloth or curled hair, and the last coat with pulverized pumice stone and crude oil or raw linseed oil.

FOR A DULL FINISH:—Specify that the last coat be rubbed with pulverized pumice stone and water, instead of oil.

FOR A POLISHED FINISH:—Specify that the last coat be rubbed first with pulverized pumice stone and water and then with pulverized rotten stone and water, and for a *piano finish* specify a further rubbing with Berry Brothers' Furniture Polish, used with a little pulverized rotten stone, applied with a piece of soft felt or flannel.

If a rubbed finish is not desired, omit the specifications for rubbing the last coat.

THE above specifications provide for finishing the wood in the natural color, but very handsome effects can be produced by staining.

If staining is required, precede the Shellac coat with a coat of Berry Brothers' Stain, "Mahogany," "Cherry," or otherwise, as may be wished.

If it is desired to finish up the wood as light as possible specify White Shellac instead of Orange Shellac and omit staining.

CYPRESS.

THIS is a close grained wood and needs no filling. For finishing in the natural color,

SPECIFY AS FOLLOWS:

FOR AN EGG SHELL GLOSS:—One coat of White Shellac sandpapered to a smooth surface, followed by two or three coats of Berry Brothers' Luxeberry Wood Finish (White or Light); rub first coats with hair cloth or curled hair, and the last with pulverized pumice stone and crude oil or raw linseed oil.

For a Dull Finish:—Specify that the last coat be rubbed with pulverized pumice stone and water, instead of oil.

For a Polished Finish:—Specify that the last coat be rubbed first with pulverized pumice stone and water and then with pulverized rotten stone and water, and for a *piano finish* specify a further rubbing with Berry Brothers' Furniture Polish, used with a little pulverized rotten stone, applied with a piece of soft felt or flannel.

If a rubbed finish is not desired, omit the specifications for rubbing the last coat.

NOTES.

IF a little deeper tone than the natural color of the wood is desired, specify Orange Shellac instead of White Shellac. Very rich effects can also be produced on Cypress by staining, individual taste governing the choice as to color.

There is a quality inherent in Cypress not met with in other woods, consisting of a peculiar greasy appearance on the surface. It is overcome in various ways by wood finishers, but we have found a second coat of Shellac, following the first, quite effective.

If the wood is to be stained, specify Orange Shellac, and precede the Shellac coat with a coat of Berry Brothers' Stain, "Cherry," "Mahogany," or otherwise, as may be desired.

PINE.

———

THIS being a close grained wood needs no filling. For finishing in the natural color,

SPECIFY AS FOLLOWS:

FOR AN EGG SHELL GLOSS:—One coat of Shellac (White Shellac if the natural color of the wood is to be preserved, or Orange Shellac if the wood is to be stained, or is desired to be darker in tone than the natural color), sandpaper to a smooth surface, and follow with two or three coats of Berry Brothers' Luxeberry Wood Finish (White or Light); specify Luxeberry Wood Finish (White) if it is desired to retain the natural color of White Pine; rub first coats with hair cloth or curled hair, and the last coat with pulverized pumice stone and crude oil or raw linseed oil.

FOR A DULL FINISH:—Specify that the last coat be rubbed with pulverized pumice stone and water, instead of oil.

FOR A POLISHED FINISH:—Specify that the last coat be rubbed first with pulverized pumice stone and water and then with pulverized rotten stone and water, and for a *piano finish* specify a further rubbing with Berry Brothers' Furniture Polish, used with a little pulverized rotten stone, applied with a piece of soft felt or flannel.

If a rubbed finish is not desired, omit the specifications for rubbing the last coat.

NOTES.

THE first coat of Shellac should never be omitted on Pine, as it serves to kill the sap or pitch, which might otherwise, in the course of time, ooze out and mar the finish.

If it is desired to retain the clear, bright color of Pine, never apply a first coat of linseed oil, as this will in time cause the wood to turn dark and present an unsightly appearance.

If the wood is to be stained, specify Orange Shellac and precede the Shellac coat with a coat of Berry Brothers' Stain of the required shade.

It may be here remarked that Georgia or Southern Pine is much more susceptible of rich and beautiful effects by staining than is White Pine.

WHITEWOOD OR POPLAR, HEMLOCK.

BOTH of these woods are close grained and need no filling.

SPECIFY AS FOLLOWS:

FOR AN EGG SHELL GLOSS:—One coat of White Shellac sandpapered to a smooth surface, followed by two or three coats of Berry Brothers' Luxeberry Wood Finish (White or Light) ; rub first coats with hair cloth or curled hair, and the last coat with pulverized pumice stone and crude or raw linseed oil.

FOR A DULL FINISH:—Specify that the last coat be rubbed with pulverized pumice stone and water instead of oil.

For a Polished Finish:—Specify that the last coat be rubbed first with pulverized pumice stone and water and then with pulverized rotten stone and water, and for a *piano finish* specify a further rubbing with Berry Brothers' Furniture Polish, used with a little pulverized rotten stone, applied with a piece of soft felt or flannel.

If a rubbed finish is not desired, omit the specifications for rubbing the last coat.

NOTES.

THESE specifications are for finishing the above woods in the natural color. If a deeper tone is desired specify Orange Shellac instead of White Shellac.

These woods are sometimes stained, individual taste dictating the shade or color.

When staining is desired, specify Orange Shellac, and precede the Shellac coat with a coat of Berry Brothers' Stain of the required shade.

FLOOR FINISHING.

F OR coarse or open grained woods,

SPECIFY AS FOLLOWS:

Fill with Berry Brothers' Paste Filler to match the color of the wood, or if the wood is stained to match the color of the stain, wipe off clean, and apply two coats of Berry Brothers' "Liquid Granite A," taking care that the first coat is thoroughly hard before applying the second; rub the second coat down with pulverized pumice stone and crude oil or raw linseed oil, and then wipe the floor perfectly dry and clean, so that no trace of oil remains to catch the dirt.

For close grained wood specify as above, but omit the filler.

NOTES.

I F color effects are wanted on floors the finishing should be preceded by staining, as directed herein for the various woods.

In using such a tough and elastic Finish as "Liquid Granite" it should be remembered that it cannot harden so quickly as varnishes possessing less elasticity, and care should be taken not to apply it too heavily or the drying will be unnecessarily retarded.

A light coat is as efficacious as a heavy coat and is always to be preferred.

For refinishing a floor and for linoleum use "Liquid Granite B."

It is well to give old linoleum a thin coat of Shellac before applying the Liquid Granite. The reason for this is that places where the original surface of the linoleum is worn off are more or less spongy, and the Shellac coat stops the suction, making a hard uniform surface to finish on.

OUTSIDE DOORS, STORE FRONTS, ETC.

F OR work of this character, if the finish is to be in natural woods,

SPECIFY AS FOLLOWS:

One coat of Berry Brothers' Paste Filler to match the color of the wood, or if stained to match the color of the stain, followed by three or four coats of Berry

Brothers' Elastic Outside Finish. Allow each coat to get thoroughly hard before applying another, and rub each coat, except the last, with hair cloth or curled hair. The last coat to be rubbed with pulverized pumice stone and oil or water in the same manner as specified for Luxeberry Wood Finish.

Although Elastic Outside Finish dries naturally to a handsome gloss, rubbing down as above directed improves the appearance and adds to the durability of the finish.

NOTES.

ONLY coarse or open grained woods need filling. On newly painted or grained work specify as above, and also add that all under coats must be thoroughly hard before applying the finish.

For old work the specifications should read the same as for newly painted or grained work, but specify in addition that before finishing, the work be well sandpapered and cleaned.

It is of the utmost importance that each and every coat is thoroughly hard before applying another, as otherwise the finish is liable to crack.

WINDOW SASH AND SILLS, BATH-ROOMS, INSIDE BLINDS, ETC.

T HE wood should lbe shellaced or filled, either or both, according to the wood to be finished, in the same manner as heretofore described, and then receive two or three coats of Berry Brothers' Elastic Interior Finish, applied and manipulated in the same manner as our Luxeberry Wood Finish.

Refer to index for wood to be finished, and word specifications in the manner directed, only substituting "Berry Brothers' Elastic Interior Finish" for "Luxeberry Wood Finish."

SHINGLES.

T O get the best results in staining shingles they should receive one dipping of *"Shingletint"* before being laid, and one brush coat after laying. It is only necessary to dip shingles two-thirds of their length.

Shingles that are laid before staining should receive not less than two coats of stain. Old shingles will take more stain than new, by reason of their greater absorbency.

The covering capacity of *Shingletint* depends upon the manner in which it is used. If brushed on, a gallon will cover 160 square feet, one coat, while 1½ gallons will cover the same surface two coats. From 2¼ to 2½ gallons is sufficient to dip 1,000 shingles, and less than a gallon more is enough for a brush coat in addition after the shingles are laid.

While using *"Shingletint"* care should be taken to keep it thoroughly stirred from the bottom, so as to keep the coloring matter in perfect suspension throughout the solvent.

DULL FINISH.

THE adoption of dull finishes on woodwork for interiors is now quite popular, the colors embracing browns, greens, reds and other shades in great variety, but while these dull effects have an undoubted artistic value, we do not consider them so beautiful as the soft richness of the egg shell gloss that Berry Brothers' Luxeberry Wood Finish has made so popular.

Most of the colors included in the various styles of finish described herein may be reproduced in the dull finish, the main feature being the entire absence of gloss.

As already explained, the finish produced with Lacklustre does not resemble a rubbed varnish effect in any way, but is more like a wax finish in appearance.

The production of the finish is quite simple, consisting merely of the application of one coat of Lacklustre with a soft brush and rubbing off with a bunch of cotton waste or piece of cheese cloth.

The covering capacity of Lacklustre is about 600 square feet to the gallon.

IMITATION RUBBED FINISH.

Where economy is a consideration and a rubbed finish effect is desired, it may be obtained by the use of a finishing coat of our Dulgloss. This useful finishing material dries naturally to a dull surface closely resembling an Egg shell gloss and makes a handsome, durable finish.

GENERAL NOTES.

———

ance
good
ce to
h on.

I T is of the utmost importance to have a clean, smooth surface if a first-class finish is desired. To this end, all finishing operations in natural woods should be commenced by sandpapering the surface to be finished until it is perfectly smooth.

Another desirable and even necessary condition for a first-class job is the temperature.

Varnish is very susceptible to atmospheric conditions and cannot dry properly in a cold room; and

ary
itions
first-
fin-

if it has been exposed to a low temperature long enough to cause it to become thick it should be allowed to stand in a warm place until it regains its normal consistency.

Reducing with turpentine may be a quicker way to prepare varnish for the brush, but it creates unnatural conditions and injures its lustre.

The proper temperature in which to spread varnish is about 70° F., and if the owner demands a first-class finish he should see that the necessary heat is supplied.

Work that is to be polished should be given not less than three coats of Luxeberry Wood Finish or varnish.

Polish
finis

A nice egg shell gloss can be produced with two coats.

Egg s
glos

The cause of many an unsatisfactory job of finishing may be traced to hurried work. The allowance of sufficient time between coats is a rule that cannot be broken without injury to the finish.

Evils
hur
wor

To paraphrase the old proverb, "Finish in haste, repent at leisure."

The object in sandpapering the first coat of Stain, as directed in the foregoing, is twofold, it smooths down the grain which has a tendency to raise more or less after the application of the Stain, and throws up the high lights by removing a portion of the Stain from the markings of the wood, thus causing them to stand out in greater contrast than they would otherwise. The second coat of Stain is diluted so that it will not obscure the grain while it deepens the color of the field or open grain of the wood. This second coat of Stain should be ap-

Why t
first
of S
is se
pap

Why t
seco
coat
Stai
dilu

plied very sparingly, and the best results are obtained by rubbing it on with a rag. Should it be necessary after the application of the second coat of Stain, a slight rubbing with polishing sandpaper will make the surface perfectly smooth for the finishing coat.

The object of preceding the filling with a light coat of thin Shellac is to protect the solid parts of the wood against discoloration by the filler. In other words, the thin film of Shellac does not fill the open grain of the wood to any appreciable extent, allowing full ingress of the filler where it is needed, while it makes an impervious coating over the solid structure, preventing the wood from absorbing the filler where it is not wanted, so that it is easily removed by a light sandpapering after the filler has become dry.

coat
hellac
cedes
filling.

It therefore enables a much cleaner job to be done than would be possible without the Shellac coat, overcoming the muddy or cloudy appearance that is sometimes seen, and enhancing the beauty of the finish by making a more distinct contrast between the high lights and low lights.

. A successful job of refinishing depends largely upon the care bestowed on cleaning off the old surface. This is accomplished in various ways, according to the condition of the finish and the desired results. If the old finish is badly checked it may be necessary to get right down to the wood in order to make a satisfactory job. A good cleaning with soap and water, followed by a judicious use of sandpaper may prove sufficient in some cases where the old finish is in fair condition. If the cleaning and sandpapering leave the surface uneven in color tone, uniformity may be restored by a careful use of Stain, or paste filler colored to the right shade and reduced to the consistency of stain with spirits of turpentine. A coat of Shellac is desirable after staining, and the finish may then be proceeded with by the application of varnish in the regular way.

Refinis
old wo

Too much emphasis cannot be given to the fact that no varnish can dry properly over a greasy surface.

Beware
greas
surfac

In refinishing church and school seats and other work of this nature, grease is always present, and unless it is entirely removed the finish will remain tacky.

Refinish
churc
and sc
seats.

It will be noticed that in the directions for using our Luxeberry Wood Finish, we invariably say, Luxeberry Wood Varnish, "White" or "Light." It is only absolutely necessary to use the Luxeberry

Wood Finish, "White" (which is almost colorless), when very light woods are to be finished in the natural color; in all other cases the "Light" may be used.

Whenever expense, however, is a secondary consideration, we always recommend the use of the Luxeberry Wood Finish "White" on any wood, as it is extra nice and well repays the small additional cost per gallon.

It is the inevitable tendency of all woods to grow darker with age, but where it is desired to preserve the natural color of the wood as long as possible, it can be done by preceding the filling,—or the varnishing when no filler is used—with a light coat of White Shellac. The reason for this is that oil applied directly to wood, causes it to turn dark, but by preceding it with a light coat of Shellac, the oil in the filler or varnish cannot penetrate the pores of the wood, which consequently retains its natural color longer than it otherwise would.

In cases where the wood is filled, the Shellac coat may be omitted if desired, but no great economy is effected thereby as at least an additional coat of Luxeberry Wood Finish (or other Finish) would be necessary to make up for such omission.

Oil and Spirit Stains possess some advantages over Water Stains, among which may be mentioned their comparative immunity from freezing, although use tends to obscure the grain of the wood more or less, and they do not produce such rich color effects as Water Stains.

Compa
tive
meri
Oil a
Wate
Stain

For staining old work Oil or Spirit Stains should always be used. The reason for this is that water stains perform their work by absorption, and in old work the porous properties of the wood are either destroyed or impaired by the previous finishing, so that the water stain cannot penetrate.

A fact worth remembering is that the same Stain will not produce exactly the same shade on all woods. The porous wood will absorb more Stain than hard, close grain woods, and consequently the color effect will be darker on the more porous wood. Hard woods with pronounced grain or markings will also take Stain in a different manner from woods showing no grain. The obvious reason for this is that the Stain penetrates more deeply into the spongy portions of the woods so that the harder parts or the grain show lighter, and consequently change the general color effect.

Same
will
prod
same
or on
woods.

The approximate covering capacity of varnish used under normal conditions is about 600 square feet to the gallon, one coat.

These figures are not arbitrary, however, as one finisher will make a given quantity of varnish cover a larger area than another, much depending upon the manner in which it is spread.

A gallon of Shellac should cover from 100 to 150 square feet more than the same quantity of varnish.

The covering capacity of water stains differs according to the wood on which it is used.

On open grained woods a gallon of water stain will cover about 650 square feet, while the same quantity on close grained hard woods would probably cover 100 square feet more surface. On soft woods a gallon of water stain will cover from 100 to 200 feet less than the above estimates, the absorbency of the wood determining the covering capacity of the stain.

Spirit stains, owing to their tendency to evaporate and strike into the wood, have a much smaller covering capacity than water stains—approximately one-half.

Oil Stains have about the same covering capacity as water stains on hard woods and will cover more surface on soft woods, as they do not absorb as water stains do. In other words, a gallon of oil stain will cover about 600 square feet or so on either hard or soft woods.

Liquid Fillers are sometimes used as first coats on close grained woods from motives of economy when shellac is considered too expensive.

They are not intended for use on open grained woods, as they are not fillers in the strict sense of the word, but first coaters, and will not fill the grain of such woods as oak, ash, chestnut, etc.

Liquid Fillers should not be used for first coats in finishing floors or fine jobs of natural wood finishing.

The covering capacity of Liquid Filler is about 250 square feet to the gallon.

In the use of Paste Filler the number of pounds to the gallon can be controlled by the finisher and is determined by the wood to be filled, the more opened grained woods requiring the filler to be heavier in body than the close grained woods.

For instance, mahogany, walnut and butternut are open grained woods, but are not nearly so open grained as oak, ash or chestnut, so that for the three first named woods the filler need not be so heavy in body as for the three last named.

The following rule for reducing paste filler for use is a good one: for oak, ash, chestnut and other very coarse grained woods, use 7 to 9 pounds to the gallon, while for mahogany, walnut, butternut and similar grained woods a mixture of 6 pounds or paste filler to the gallon will be found sufficient.

The covering capacity of paste filler reduced for use is about 300 square feet to the gallon when used on work where no waste occurs.

We invite inquiries from any who may desire information on wood finishing, and as Varnish Manufacturers of nearly fifty years' experience, we may without affectation claim to be competent authority on the subject.

We keep on hand finished specimens of the various woods used for interior finishing purposes, which we will mail, post paid, to any address, or we will finish up any samples of wood that may be sent to us for the purpose, returning same with explicit instructions as to the mode of finishing.

BERRY BROTHERS, Limited.

CONDENSED FACTS ON COVERING CAPACITIES.

A gallon of varnish will cover approximately 600 sq. feet, one coat.

A gallon of Shellac will cover from 700 to 750 sq. feet.

A gallon of Water Stain covers about 650 sq. feet on open-grained woods, and on close-grained hard woods, 100 sq. feet more. On soft woods a gallon of Water Stain will cover from 400 to 500 sq. feet.

A gallon of Spirit Stain will cover from 300 to 400 square feet, according to the wood.

A gallon of Oil Stain will cover about 600 sq. feet on all woods.

A gallon of Paste Filler reduced for use covers about 300 sq. feet, and from seven to nine pounds of paste filler are required to make a gallon.

A gallon of Shingletint covers about 160 feet, one coat, if brushed on; 1½ gallons covers the same surface, two coats. From 2¼ to 2½ gallons will dip 1,000 shingles, and another gallon is enough for a brush coat in addition after the shingles are laid.

CPSIA information can be obtained
at www.ICGtesting.com
Printed in the USA
BVHW081833191118
533513BV00022B/1114/P